How To Get Into The Real Ball Game Of Politics Where You Live To Help President Donald J. Trump Make America Great Again

DANIEL J. SCHULTZ

DEDICATION

This book is dedicated to my beautiful, loving wife and my wonderful children who have patiently and lovingly put up with my efforts to engage greater numbers of conservatives to get involved in Republican Party politics where they live and to the late Sam Alvord, who taught me basic American Civics in junior high school in the late 1960s in Alma, Wisconsin.

CONTENTS

ACKNOWLEDGMENTS

I would like to thank all of the wonderful conservatives I have met since actively getting involved in party politics at the precinct and local committee level back in 2007 in Tempe, Arizona from whom I have learned so much about how to help conservatives get elected to party officer positions and to public office.

1 FOREWORD

This book is for conservatives who are tired of being lied to by fake Republicans who run as "Campaign Conservatives" (in the words of Texas Senator Ted Cruz) and who want to do something to "change" these fake Republicans by taking them out of their current office in the upcoming 2018 primary elections and beyond. The only conservatives that matter are those we conservatives succeed in electing to office, and this book will teach you how to get into the fray to make that happen. It happens, simply put, when the best conservative in the all-important, traditionally-very-low-turnout primary elections, gets more votes than the other Republican primary election candidates.

I recently re-read Sen. Barry Goldwater's "The Conscience of a Conservative" because I wanted to see if it had anything in it that related to how conservatives could

organize and unite politically for real political action where

they live to elect the conservatives necessary to achieve the

goals of the book. I had purchased the book in the mid-

1980s while on Army Reserve duty at Fort Huachuca,

Arizona, at a used book store. The fifth and sixth

paragraphs said this:

And so the question arises:

Why have American people

been unable to translate their

views into appropriate political

action? Why should the

nation's underlying allegiance

to Conservative principles have

failed to produce

corresponding deeds in Washington?

I do not blame my brethren in government, all of whom work hard and conscientiously at their jobs. *I blame Conservatives—ourselves—myself. Our failure, as one Conservative writer has put it, is the failure of the Conservative* **demonstration**. Though we Conservatives are deeply persuaded that our society is ailing, and know that Conservatism holds the key to national salvation—and feel sure the country agrees with us—*we seem unable to*

demonstrate *the practical*

relevance of Conservative principles to

the needs of the day. We sit by

impotently while Congress

seeks to improvise solutions to

problems that are not the real

problems facing the country,

while the government attempts

to assuage imagined concerns

and ignores the real concerns

and real needs of the people.

("The Conscience of a Conservative," Goldwater, Barry,

Foreword, Victor Publishing Company, Inc. (1960); italics

and bolding added.)

I found no further discussion in this otherwise excellent book about how conservatives ought to "demonstrate" how to make sure conservative principles actually become practically relevant to the needs of the day. However, Sen. Goldwater touched upon the solution, in Chapter Two, stating, regarding what the framers of our Constitution knew, "In the last analysis their system of government would prosper only if the governed were sufficiently determined that it should. 'What have you given us?' a woman asked Ben Franklin toward the close of the Constitutional Convention? 'A Republic,' he said, '*if you can keep it!*'"

This book fills that gap. It will tell you how conservatives can "demonstrate the practical relevance of Conservative principles to the needs of the day." This book, if you do the few concrete things outlined in it, will negate the possibility, if ever asked by your children, "Why didn't you do something, when you had the time and the

resources, to stop America's slide into socialism?", of

having to say, "I'm sorry, I just did not know what to do."

Let us keep our Republic, shall we? This book tells you

how to keep it. But—and this is a big but—it will take

physical action on your part and on the part of many other

conservatives you know. And here's some good news.

You will enjoy doing this. It will be meaningful to you.

You will meet some very interesting people – some very

good people, and probably some not so very good people.

The idea is to do what is necessary to get the good people

to outnumber the not good people, because in party

politics the fundamental rule is the majority rules. If we

can build a majority of good people in our Party's

apparatus, at the precinct level, we will have a good political

party.

We have a country and a civilization to save. Are you up for it? You are. You, dear reader, are the key. You are one of the "We the People." I pray you will immediately act.

Thank you. Daniel J. Schultz.

2 THIS BOOK IS FOR CONSERVATIVES WHO WANT TO DO SOMETHING

Right now, by my estimates, fewer than one out of every two hundred and fifty Republicans are engaged where they live in the actual operating apparatus of the Republican Party. In a nutshell, that lack of active participation defines our political problem. If you want to be one of the warm bodies that will get involved, where you live, in Republican Party politics (this book will explain what that means), then read on. But, if you are unwilling to gather about ten signatures on a nomination form, or are unwilling to occasionally attend a local Party committee meeting, and are unwilling to spend three hours or so at the time of the primary and then the general election making a few phone calls to fellow Republicans and dropping off candidate information at maybe forty or fifty doors (you

won't have to ring any door bells or knock on any doors),
then you may as well stop reading, as this book is not for
you.

And therein lies the problem. Not enough
conservatives are willing to participate in our political
process in this manner. Over half of these voting-precinct
level Party slots go begging for a warm conservative body.
Approximately four hundred thousand of these internal
Party slots exist, and over half of them are vacant. If we
can get about two hundred thousand conservatives to fill
up these vacant slots, we conservatives will *be* the Party.

If you do keep reading, and do the things I hope you
will do, you will become part of the approximately one out
of one hundred and twenty-five Republicans who are
allowed to participate in the Party at local and county
committee meetings to elect the committee chairmen and
who elect the state chairman, the national committeeman

and national committeewoman of your state party, and

your state party's presidential nominating convention

delegates (these processes vary from state to state, but all

must meet requirements that the one hundred and sixty-

eight members of the Republican National Committee put

into their Rules of the Republican Party).

In other words, if you do the few simple acts I

outline in the next chapter, you will do one thing for sure

and maybe another: You will become an "elite player" in

the real ball game of politics, political party politics, and

you may be part of the army of new conservative players in

the Republican Party who will transform our Party from a

half-strength, ideologically-split party with no cohesive

conservative message into a full-strength, solidly

conservative party that will help greater numbers of

conservative candidates defeat the Republican In Name

Only fake Republicans in the all-important, traditionally-very-low-turnout primary elections – which, by the way, is the first election every incumbent must win to go on to the general election.

So, you have reached a decision point. Do you waste your time reading about things you will never do, or do you embrace the notion of empowering yourself and other conservatives to help "make America great again?"

3 THE BASIC STRATEGY IS SIMPLE

I cannot seem to recall who said it, or the exact quote, but I once read that some wise person said sometimes the solution to a seemingly hard, complex problem is very simple, and the only hard part is carrying out the simple solution. That is what we conservatives face with the current apparatus of the Republican Party.

A simple solution exists for conservatives to finally unite and organize for real political action and for taking political power away from the fake Republicans who pretend to be conservatives but always act like Democrats. I call the strategy The Neighborhood Precinct Committeeman Strategy for a reason: it starts in our respective "political neighborhoods," our voting precincts in which we live.

If I provided you with a strategy and plan that only took a couple of hours of your time every month and then three or four hours at primary and general election times, and that guaranteed increased voter turnout for the best conservative candidates, would you at least consider investing that amount of time for that desired outcome? If so, please read on.

Using this strategy, and investing a couple of hours a month, and three or four at the time of the primary and general elections, I've been able to, in my precinct, with my conservative cohorts, double Republican turnout in a local mayoral race, as compared to the city-wide average turnout for all voters, and achieve an 86+% Republican voter turnout in the 2012 general election. If conservative Republicans had done what we did in every precinct in America, Mitt Romney would have been handed a landslide victory by conservatives despite his campaign's failure to spend money on a "boots on the ground" Get Out The Vote (GOTV) strategy and plan.

Additionally, using this strategy, we conservatives have completely changed the Republican Party in terms of who has been elected to the Party local district, county, and state committee officer positions. More on that below, but let's get back to how to win the elections.

So, what's the key for changing the outcome of elections? And, at the same time, transforming the Republican Party into a conservative election-winning powerhouse? The key is YOU. Where you live. With other conservatives.

The key is you and your fellow conservatives attending your local Republican Party committee meeting every month (that takes about two hours a month) where you can learn how to become a voting member of the

Party—a precinct committeeman.

http://www.unifiedpatriots.com/2013/04/29/want-to-do-something-heres-an-11-minute-vid-that-tells-you-what-to-do-and-more/ (You don't have to attend every meeting; you will learn which meetings are the critical ones.) Then, in the weeks leading up to the primary and general elections, you will be in a position, using the GOP Data Center software provided by the Republican National Committee to the state parties (or whatever new software they might be providing, if any (more on that later)), to target the "lower information, lower propensity" (I call them "Voters In Name Only, or VINOs (vy noes)) Republican voters and gently nudge them to the polls with a quick, personal phone call followed up by a literature drop consisting of a filled out sample ballot and literature provided by the Republican candidates. Many of these conservative Republican voters, who do not pay too much attention to politics, will turn out to vote if they are gently reminded about the importance of their primary election votes and give them a sample ballot that will tell them which candidates are the conservative candidates (and perhaps, also, some candidate literature).

In the 2012 mayoral race in my city, Tempe, Arizona, using this strategy, my fellow conservative precinct committeemen and I, each investing just three to four hours of time, doubled Republican turnout in our precinct as compared to the city-wide turnout of all voters. City elections, by statute, in Arizona (with exceptions), are "non-partisan;" that is, the election ballot does not identify for the voters the candidates' respective political party affiliation. Thus, many "lower information" Republican voters do not know which candidates to vote for. That is where the precinct committeemen can fill the gap. Using the GOP Data Center software, those who vote 50% or less of the time in past elections can be identified and targeted. That is about 35% of the Republican voters. Unlike the VINOs, we did not bother contacting those who voted 75% or 100% of the time because they were very likely to vote without a gentle "nudge" from us. We only had limited resources, so we wanted to target our efforts to Republican voters who normally do not vote in the primary elections.

Using this same strategy and plan, in the 2012 general election, as I already mentioned, we achieved a Republican turnout of 86+% in my precinct as compared to a state-wide average of 74% turnout. Again, if we conservatives had organized and united for real political action where we live, "inside" the Republican Party as precinct committeemen, and then carried out our own GOTV efforts, we would have won the election for Mitt Romney despite his reluctance to recruit conservatives into the precinct committeeman ranks for these GOTV efforts

(as I had advised him and his campaign to do).

By conservatives becoming Republican Party

precinct committeemen, not only will we start down the

path to winning elections for our conservative Republican

candidates in the all-important, traditionally-very-low-

turnout primary elections, and then the general elections,

but we'll also be in a position to elect greater numbers of

conservatives to the officer slots of the Party. Currently, it's

estimated about 400,000 Republican Party precinct

committeeman slots exist nationwide. Only about 200,000

of these slots are filled. And they're split, approximately 50-

50, between conservatives and moderates. We see the effect

of that split manifested every two years when the

Republican National Committee ("RNC") Chairman is

elected by the RNC members (consisting of the state

chairman and one national committeeman and one national

committeewoman from each state). Rather than having a

true conservative fighter elected, we have gotten the likes

of Michael Steele and Reince Priebus – they say they are

conservatives, but sure don't act like conservatives, in my

humble opinion. Actions speak louder than words.

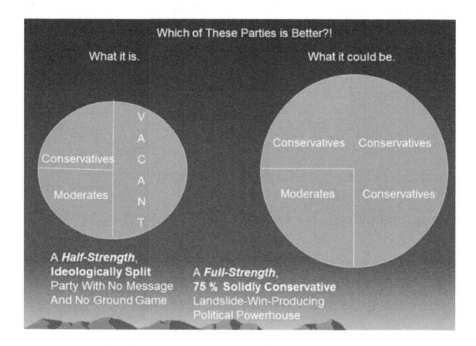

Who elects the RNC members? Indirectly, the

precinct committeemen elect them. Precinct

committeemen *are* the Party.

For example, in Arizona the precinct committeemen in each of the thirty legislative district committees elect, every two years, one state committeeman for every three precinct committeemen in their district (which is an incentive for the conservative precinct committeemen in each district to recruit more conservatives into the vacant precinct committeeman slots). These state committeemen attend an annual state committee meeting where they elect the state chairman and the other officers. Every four years, the precinct committeemen in each legislative district elect delegates to the state presidential nominating convention. Those delegates elect the national committeeman and the national committeewoman. So, the greater number of elected conservative precinct committeemen the Party has, the greater likelihood the state chairman and the national committeeman and national committeewoman will be conservatives.

Majority rules. Create a conservative majority of precinct committeeman in your local Party committee, and you will be able to elect conservative committee officers.

Many conservatives complain about "the Republican Party." That it is not "conservative enough" and that the Republicans in the U.S. Senate and House do not follow the Party platform. They are correct. But the blame does not lie with "the Republican Party." It lies with those conservatives who will not become precinct committeemen. The reason the Republican Party fails to be "conservative enough," and fails in electing more conservatives to office, is because not enough of those same complaining conservative Republicans are "in" the Party as precinct committeemen helping to get out the vote in the primary elections for the most conservative candidates and making the Party itself "more conservative" and "conservative enough" for their liking. Plato said those who fail to participate in politics are destined to be

ruled by their inferiors. Are we not now being ruled by our

inferiors? You Are willing to participate in politics to

change that? I hope and pray so.

Here in Arizona, after the 2008 primary election,

only about one-third of the allotted Republican Party

precinct committeeman slots were filled and those filled

slots were split about 50-50 between conservatives and

moderates. That ideological split was reflected in the

elected officer ranks of the legislative district committees,

the county committees, and the state committee. Because,

after the election of President Obama, I and other

conservatives began recruiting conservative Republicans at

tea party gatherings, 9.12 group meetings, etc., we had

swelled the PC ranks in Maricopa County to about 55%

strength and almost completely "changed out" the

moderates in the Party committee officer ranks. This strategy works.

Here in Arizona, by statute, each political party gets one precinct committeeman slot for each precinct and then an additional one for every 125 registered voters of the party residing in the precinct – or majority portion thereof. My current precinct has eleven precinct committeeman slots, and all eleven are filled with conservatives. We've divided the precinct into eleven sectors, and we are each responsible for a sector. Because we only target the 35% of the voters who fall into the "low propensity to vote" category, it only takes us a few hours at the time of the primary and general election to call them and provide them with a sample ballot and candidate literature. Our GOTV strategy works. It is just common sense.

And how does one become a precinct committeeman? The requirements vary in each state, but none are onerous. Here in Arizona, the registered voters of each party elect their precinct committeemen in the even-numbered year primary elections. To get on the ballot, a precinct committeeman candidate must gather just ten signatures or fewer from registered voters of his party or non-affiliated voters. The fewer registered Republicans in the precinct, the lower the number of signatures needed. In one precinct in which I recruited precinct committeeman candidates, only three signatures were needed. As one signature can be of the candidate, the candidate needed only two signatures. The husband and wife I recruited signed for themselves and each other and then went to a friendly neighbor to get their third signatures.

The Party will supply the candidate with the nominating petition and a walking sheet for his precinct identifying those houses containing registered members of his party and the non-affiliated voters. It takes me about 45 minutes to gather the ten signatures. I've compiled what I've been able to find on the internet regarding each state's requirements here.

https://theprecinctproject.wordpress.com/

There's a reason precinct committeeman has been called "The Most Powerful Political Office in the World"– because it really is.

http://eagleforum.org/misc/brochures/precinct-committman.shtml And if conservatives would organize and unite where they live, inside the Republican Party, by becoming voting members of the Republican Party – precinct committeemen – we'd begin the process of restoring our Republic as envisioned by our Founding Fathers. Because about half of these precinct committeeman slots are vacant, on average, in every locale, the Party is there for the taking by conservatives if conservatives will fill up all the vacant precinct

committeeman slots.

So why haven't you heard about this? Because most

incumbents, even the conservative incumbents, have a

vested interest in maintaining the status quo inside the

Party. If everything stays the same, they'll probably win

their next primary election and then the general election. If

they recruit more conservatives into the vacant precinct

committeeman slots, they might sow the seeds of their own

primary election destruction if someone "more

conservative" than they are runs against them.

All politics truly are local, and, therefore, most

"national" advocacy groups would prefer you not discover

this fact. Your time and money is best spent where you live,

increasing voter turnout through the best, most effective

method: neighbor-to-neighbor by calling your fellow

Republicans in your precinct and then dropping off a sample ballot and candidate literature to help them make informed votes. And changing the Party from within— making it "more conservative" by increasing the number of conservatives "inside it."

Simply put, as mentioned above, the reason the Republican Party is not "conservative enough" for some complaining conservatives is because not enough of those same complaining conservatives are "inside" the Republican Party where they live—as precinct committeemen.

You can carve out a couple of hours a month to do this, no? And three or four hours at the time of the primary and general elections, no? For your future and your kids' and grandkids' futures?

You can.

And I hope and pray you will. (Plus, it's fun and

interesting. Really. And personally rewarding in many ways

as you will discover.)

So now you know what to do.

4 THE KEY POSITIONS IN OUR PARTY – "IT'S THE CHAIRMEN, STUPID!"

I put, "It's the Chairmen, Stupid!" in quotes because I never liked the "It's [whatever], stupid!" phrase because I don't like to call people stupid. But, that phrase does seem to grab attention. And allows me to segue[1] to an obvious point about political party politics, one I was too "stupid" to grasp for many years: Working back from the Rules of the Republican Party, down to the state committees and their respective state committee bylaws, and then down to the county committees and their respective county

---

[1] I hate "politispeak." Every month or so the "chattering class" "talking heads" (these two phrases are examples of politispeak) in Washington, D.C., somehow generate the use of some new term or obscure word to show those who do not live "inside the Beltway" (another such term invented by them long ago) that they are not insiders because they do not know all the "insider" language. Because they are unable to utter sentences like:
The *sina qua non* of the billionaire writ large Donald Trump's unspoken attempt to create a meme and aura of gravitas has been his tranche of bespoke pin-striped suits; there will never be a segue into a discussion by any talking head self-appointed so-called thought-leaders with him about talking points relating to a clown car homebrew server because such a thing would never be the *piece de resistance* within his wheelhouse.

committee bylaws, and then down to the local Party

committees, and their respective committee bylaws, the

rules/bylaws of these committees make clear that the most

important positions are the Party committee chairmen

positions. Period. They have, and must have, almost

dictatorial powers because, if that were not so, nothing

would get accomplished. If sub-committees of these

committees ran things, or if the other officers of the

committees ran things, nothing would ever get

accomplished, because everything that needed to be done

would get "committee-ed to death." So, from the local

committees all the way "up" (or "down," if you share my

perspective) to the RNC, the committee chairman has

virtually unfettered authority to carry out the business of

the committee.

One check on the power of the chairman exists: the

threat of removal by the members of the committee. That

check is hard to orchestrate, unless the members of the committee are communicating effectively and efficiently via either email or some Party-supplied software. Hint: The RNC will *never* provide such software to the precinct committeemen in the states, because to do so would empower the precinct committeemen and state committeemen to easily communicate with one another to remove those chairmen who do destructive things to the Party.

The good news: The costs of these communication tools is coming down, down, down. Investigate NationBuilder, Voter Gravity, and rVotes. Free tools include Facebook, which has Secret Groups where only invited members will see what is being discussed. Again, please do not wait on the RNC Establishment fake Republicans to deliver to you this kind of communication tool. Just do it yourself.

And, then, make sure that when you are voting for committee officers, or the people who will vote for the committee officers, you spend the most time learning everything you can about the beliefs of the chairmen candidates. Try to figure out if they really do hold conservative beliefs or just pretend to do so. Talk to as many people you trust who might know the candidates. Talk to the candidates themselves if you can, and ask them hard questions about their beliefs.

Again, the most important, most powerful, elected officials in the Republican Party apparatus are the RNC chairman, the state committee chairmen, the county committee chairmen, and the local Party committee chairmen. All of whom, directly or indirectly, the precinct committeemen of the Party elect.

5 THE ESTABLISHMENT WILL NEVER GIVE US WHAT WE NEED – SO WE NEED TO GET IT OURSELVES

I was foolish. After I became an appointed precinct

committeeman in 2007, and then an elected precinct

committeeman in 2008, I began to learn that precinct

committeemen had no way to communicate with one

another electronically. The RNC and the National

Republican Senatorial Committee ("NRSC") and the

National Republican Congressional Committee ("NRCC")

had the wherewithal to email those Republicans for whom

they had an email address, to ask for money, but they did

not know, for example, that I was an elected precinct

committeeman – even though the Maricopa County

Recorder publishes online a downloadable spreadsheet of

all of the elected precinct committeemen in the county and

then updates it periodically as new people are added

through the appointment process.

So, despite being an elected precinct committeeman "inside" the Party, I would receive emails from the RNC, the NRSC, and the NRCC, asking me to "join" the Party by becoming a "Sustaining Member" of their respective committee if only I would send them fifty dollars or so. Indirectly telling me that they were not bothering to cross-check their data base entries against the compilations of precinct committeemen in those counties that compile such data electronically and make it available to the public.

I asked our then state chairman why the RNC was not providing us with the kind of software the precinct committeemen needed to communicate with one another for getting out the vote, recruiting additional precinct committeemen, etc. The answer was: Be patient. It is coming. Michael Steele came and went, and the software never came. Reince Priebus came and went, and the software never came.

We still have no such Party software.

Luckily, as already mentioned in the preceding chapter, many free or inexpensive tools exist for conservative precinct committeemen to begin building electronic networks on which they can communicate. Find a tool that works for you and start adding those conservatives you know to your communications network. Ask them to collaborate with you to make it secure and private. Thereby creating conservative caucuses among your fellow precinct committeemen in your precinct, within your local committee, within your county committee, and within your state committee. Because as long as the RNC has a majority of non-conservatives on it, it will have no interest in giving you such a tool.

6 WHY THE ESTABLISHMENT, AND EVEN MOST CONSERVATIVE PRIMARY CANDIDATES, WILL NOT TELL YOU WHY AND HOW TO BECOME A PRECINCT COMMITTEEMAN

The Republican Party Establishment will never breathe a word about the fact that, on average, across the country, over half of the precinct committeeman slots are vacant in every precinct.

So why have you not you heard about this from incumbent Republicans? Because most incumbents, even the conservative incumbents, have a vested interest in maintaining the status quo inside the Party. If everything stays the same, they will probably win their next primary election and then the general election.

As for the conservative primary election candidates, almost all are afraid to tell conservatives about the how and why of becoming a precinct committeeman to support them because they fear those new conservative precinct committeemen might end up supporting some other conservative candidate. If they recruit more conservatives into the vacant precinct committeeman slots, they might sow the seeds of their own primary election destruction if someone "more conservative" than they are ends up running against them in a future primary.

And why don't you ever get a mailer from a "conservative" group asking for donations that also tells you about the how and why of becoming a precinct committeeman? Because they know this truism: all politics are local. Therefore, these "national" advocacy groups would prefer you not discover this fact. Your time and money is best spent where you live, increasing voter turnout through the best, most effective method: neighbor-to-neighbor by calling your fellow Republicans in your precinct and then dropping off a sample ballot and candidate literature to help them make informed votes.

And changing the Party from within – making it "more

conservative" by increasing the number of conservatives

"inside it."

If these groups were to tell you about how to really

help empower yourself locally with other conservatives

where you live, then you might figure out that your money

is better spent where you live. In other words, telling you

how best to spend your time and money, your political

capital, locally, does not serve their financial best interests.

They are in the business of convincing you, via fund-raising

letters, to send your money to the "expert political

operatives" who will somehow – never guaranteed – fix

whatever political problem they believe you believe must be

fixed.

Spend your time and money on political action locally. The best way to do so is by getting involved in the Party as a precinct committeeman.

7 ORGANIZE AND UNITE LOCALLY; WIN LOCALLY AND NATIONALLY

By organizing and uniting locally, where we each live, with other conservatives in the natural, best place to do so – our respective local Republican Party committees -- we will naturally get better at devising get out the vote strategies for winning the important local elections, such as school board races, city council races, and county board races.

Our children are our future, and we conservatives do not spend enough time and energy (well, at least this conservative is willing to admit it) finding out who the candidates are for the local school board and for city council and mayor and for the county committee. But if we did, and started helping get out the vote for the best, most conservative candidates, and started winning these races, the mechanics for winning all the other elections for conservatives would be in place.

By organizing and uniting "inside" our Republican Party at the precinct level and on our local Party committees, to get out the vote for conservatives in the local elections, we would start winning locally. And, by organizing and uniting in this way locally across the country, we would also win at the state level and the national level.

Organize and unite locally; win locally and nationally.

8 ANOTHER REASON TO ACT NOW

President Trump needs conservatives to help him get as many conservatives elected to the United States House of Representatives and the United States Senate in 2018 and beyond to help him achieve the campaign promises he made to Repeal and Replace Obamacare, build the barrier on our southern border with Mexico, stop illegal immigration, combat fundamentalist Islamic terror, reduce income tax rates, and rebuild our armed forces, to name a few of his promises. As we have already seen since President Trump assumed the office of the presidency, despite the Republican Party having a majority of the seats in both the Senate and the House of Representatives, the Republican "leaders" have failed to repeal Obamacare or pass a tax reform bill.

The Republican Establishment has a lot of money to spend on political advertising, and, perhaps, if they read this book, they may now throw some of it at efforts to fill up all the vacant precinct committeeman positions.

There are other groups that might focus on doing this, too. The immensely wealthy Koch brothers, Charles and David, thankfully have decided to not "invade" the Republican Party by filling up the precinct committeeman slots with the volunteers of their Americans for Prosperity chapters. Instead, they tell their volunteers to remain non-partisan and outside the political parties and they strive to reach their goals by educating the public about bad incumbents.

Libertarians have tried to infiltrate the Republican Party by becoming precinct committeemen, but their numbers are relatively tiny and the positions they advocate, such as an isolationist foreign policy, open borders, and the legalization of illicit drugs, cause them to fail to make much

of an impact in the Party's precinct committeeman ranks.

It has been said that trying to organize conservatives is like

herding cats. It may be that trying to herd libertarians is

like trying to herd kittens.

The graphic below shows how if a small percentage

of like-minded conservatives from various conservative

groups would decide to become precinct committeemen

where they live to fill up the vacant precinct committeeman

slots they would fundamentally transform the make-up of

the Party.

Do not procrastinate. Act now. So we can start

winning, together, now.

9 THEY DO NOT TEACH THIS ANYMORE IN PUBLIC SCHOOL, SO YOU NEED TO TEACH YOUR CHILDREN

Have you looked at your children's school curriculum? Do they get a Basic American Civics course to teach them what is set forth in this book? I have looked at the curriculum outlines for the State of Arizona's public schools. In every case, where the students would ordinarily be told what they could do to get involved in a political party, the curriculum guide says something like this: "Allow the students to engage in a guided discussion regarding what activities they might engage in to effect political change." In other words, let the students, who know nothing about political parties and how they operate, figure out on their own, if they can, that subject, instead of telling them what they need to know.

So how to reverse this? Well, one way is to have them read this book. It lays out the basics, as you now know, for how conservatives can best organize and unite for real political action in an efficient and effective manner to change the outcome of the elections both for the public offices and the internal political party offices.

Sit your children down and explain to them that if they want to keep America as it is, and make it better, that we all must spend a little bit of time and take a little bit of action, for at least a few hours every year, to make that happen. The Framers of the Constitution made explicitly clear to us by beginning the Preamble of the Constitution with the words "We the People" in large text, and then explaining that we the people are the guardians of the Constitution and that it is our job to elect representatives who will take care that the powers therein granted, and only those powers, shall be faithfully executed.

We the People of the United States, in Order to form a more perfect Union, establish Justice, insure domestic Tranquility, provide for the common defence, promote the general Welfare, and secure the Blessings of Liberty to ourselves and our Posterity, do ordain and establish this Constitution for the United States of America.

In the words of Benjamin Franklin, as he departed the Constitutional Convention, we will have a Republic if we can keep it. Please be one of the people who will help me keep it.

10 RESOURCES

Since I became involved in party politics where I live in 2007, I have met hundreds of great conservatives who also "get" The Neighborhood Precinct Committeeman Strategy and who also have been trying to convince other great conservatives to unite and organize inside the Republican Party where they live to try to take our Party apparatus away from the fake Republicans and "Campaign Conservatives" who campaign as conservatives but then govern, if elected, as Democrats. Some have pulled together information as I have in hard copy writings and on internet web pages, or in online radio interviews and informational video presentations. I have placed a variety of talks I have made onto YouTube, and those links will appear below. Here are some other great resources to learn more about how and why conservatives need to organize and unite "inside" our Party by becoming voting members of our Party's local party committees.

The Voices of America: thevoicesofamerica.org

The Madison Project: http://www.precinctproject.us/

rVotes campaign software: www.rVotes.com

Unified Patriots: www.unifiedpatriots.com

Video presentations of The Neighborhood Precinct Committeeman Strategy by the author:

February 11, 2011 talk to the Glendale, AZ Tea Party Patriots:

http://youtu.be/-dSd8kjPz5Y

http://youtu.be/ZtjCYAzzjUA

http://youtu.be/jQmfH_1I06A

http://youtu.be/Z5SKp9WDLkI

http://youtu.be/CAQUYI0SWB0

An article at UnifiedPatriots.com that links to a narrated PowerPoint video of how to use the Republican National Committee's GOP Data Center to effective increase Republican voter turnout in a precinct:

http://www.unifiedpatriots.com/2012/08/18/how-to-get-the-republican-vinos-to-the-polls-in-november/cold-warrior

Here are links to a more general "Political Activism" presentation the author gave at an American Majority event in Phoenix, Arizona in 2011:

2011 05-07 1 Political Activism

http://youtu.be/C7ASRkUPGEU

2011-05-17 2 Political Activism

http://youtu.be/FA_icUFDh28

2011 05 07 3 Political Activism http://youtu.be/q9NE-WU8c1c

2011 05 07 4 Political Activism

http://youtu.be/c1iM5H73Zbo

2011 05 07 5 Political Activism http://youtu.be/0d-CLWpRZZg

2011 05 07 6 Political Activism

http://youtu.be/wVSKoPEFJr0

2011 05 07 7 Political Activism

http://youtu.be/XrYZtBf9-Gw

2011 05 07 8 Political Activism

http://youtu.be/duU2l17UgXw

For comic relief, back in 2011, progressive Thom

Hartmann at Russia Today television stumbled upon some

of the work some of us had done via The Concord Project

to put together a web site, with tutorial videos, about The

Neighborhood Precinct Committeeman Strategy:

https://www.youtube.com/watch?v=FnHvrmjGnaU

Here are the direct links to those tutorial videos:

Concord Project GOTV – It is easy to go door to door

http://youtu.be/B90PXfj0wGY

Concord Project GOTV - How to go door to door

http://youtu.be/UTjrMifILfk

Concord Project GOTV what is a precinct and how does it

work

http://youtu.be/KMBa713YCUI

Concord Project GOTV - how you become a precinct committeeman

http://youtu.be/yMkTdMXwhbE

Concord Project GOTV - the importance of precinct committeemen

http://youtu.be/Nczt5cN8hd4

Concord Project GOTV - the time commitment for a precinct committeeman

http://youtu.be/MendmDZ-iu0

And, for convenient reference, I am including in this book the two key founding documents you should read over, and over, and over again. By now you should know which two: The Declaration of Independence and our Constitution.

The Declaration of Independence

IN CONGRESS, JULY 4, 1776

The unanimous Declaration of the thirteen united States of America

When in the Course of human events it becomes necessary for one people to dissolve the political bands which have connected them with another and to assume among the powers of the earth, the separate and equal station to which the Laws of Nature and of Nature's God entitle them, a decent respect to the opinions of mankind requires that they should declare the causes which impel them to the separation.

We hold these truths to be self-evident, that all men are created equal, that they are endowed by their Creator with certain unalienable Rights, that among these are Life, Liberty and the pursuit of Happiness. — That to secure these rights, Governments are instituted among Men, deriving their just powers from the consent of the governed, — That whenever any Form of Government becomes destructive of these ends, it is the Right of the People to alter or to abolish it, and to institute new

Government, laying its foundation on such principles and organizing its powers in such form, as to them shall seem most likely to effect their Safety and Happiness. Prudence, indeed, will dictate that Governments long established should not be changed for light and transient causes; and accordingly all experience hath shewn that mankind are more disposed to suffer, while evils are sufferable than to right themselves by abolishing the forms to which they are accustomed. But when a long train of abuses and usurpations, pursuing invariably the same Object evinces a design to reduce them under absolute Despotism, it is their right, it is their duty, to throw off such Government, and to provide new Guards for their future security. — Such has been the patient sufferance of these Colonies; and such is now the necessity which constrains them to alter their former Systems of Government. The history of the present King of Great Britain is a history of repeated injuries and usurpations, all having in direct object the establishment of an absolute Tyranny over these States. To prove this, let Facts be submitted to a candid world.

He has refused his Assent to Laws, the most wholesome and necessary for the public good.

He has forbidden his Governors to pass Laws of immediate and pressing importance, unless suspended in their operation till his Assent should be obtained; and when so suspended, he has utterly neglected to attend to them.

He has refused to pass other Laws for the accommodation of large districts of people, unless those people would relinquish the right of Representation in the Legislature, a right inestimable to them and formidable to tyrants only.

He has called together legislative bodies at places unusual, uncomfortable, and distant from the depository of their Public Records, for the sole purpose of fatiguing them into compliance with his measures.

He has dissolved Representative Houses repeatedly, for opposing with manly firmness his invasions on the rights of the people.

He has refused for a long time, after such dissolutions, to cause others to be elected, whereby the Legislative Powers, incapable of Annihilation, have returned to the People at large for their exercise; the State remaining in the mean time exposed to all the dangers of invasion from without, and convulsions within.

He has endeavoured to prevent the population of these States; for that purpose obstructing the Laws for Naturalization of Foreigners; refusing to pass others to encourage their migrations hither, and raising the conditions of new Appropriations of Lands.

He has obstructed the Administration of Justice by refusing his Assent to Laws for establishing Judiciary Powers.

He has made Judges dependent on his Will alone for the

tenure of their offices, and the amount and payment of their salaries.

He has erected a multitude of New Offices, and sent hither swarms of Officers to harass our people and eat out their substance.

He has kept among us, in times of peace, Standing Armies without the Consent of our legislatures.

He has affected to render the Military independent of and superior to the Civil Power.

He has combined with others to subject us to a jurisdiction foreign to our constitution, and unacknowledged by our laws; giving his Assent to their Acts of pretended Legislation:

For quartering large bodies of armed troops among us:

For protecting them, by a mock Trial from punishment for any Murders which they should commit on the Inhabitants of these States:

For cutting off our Trade with all parts of the world:

For imposing Taxes on us without our Consent:

For depriving us in many cases, of the benefit of Trial by Jury:

For transporting us beyond Seas to be tried for pretended offences:

For abolishing the free System of English Laws in a neighbouring Province, establishing therein an Arbitrary government, and enlarging its Boundaries so as to render it at once an example and fit instrument for introducing the same absolute rule into these Colonies

For taking away our Charters, abolishing our most valuable Laws and altering fundamentally the Forms of our Governments:

For suspending our own Legislatures, and declaring themselves invested with power to legislate for us in all cases whatsoever.

He has abdicated Government here, by declaring us out of his Protection and waging War against us.

He has plundered our seas, ravaged our coasts, burnt our towns, and destroyed the lives of our people.

He is at this time transporting large Armies of foreign Mercenaries to compleat the works of death, desolation, and tyranny, already begun with circumstances of Cruelty & Perfidy scarcely paralleled in the most barbarous ages, and totally unworthy the Head of a civilized nation.

He has constrained our fellow Citizens taken Captive on the high Seas to bear Arms against their Country, to become the executioners of their friends and Brethren, or to fall themselves by their Hands.

He has excited domestic insurrections amongst us, and has endeavoured to bring on the inhabitants of our frontiers, the merciless Indian Savages whose known rule of warfare, is an undistinguished destruction of all ages, sexes and conditions.

In every stage of these Oppressions We have Petitioned for Redress in the most humble terms: Our repeated Petitions have been answered only by repeated injury. A Prince, whose character is thus marked by every act which may define a Tyrant, is unfit to be the ruler of a free people.

Nor have We been wanting in attentions to our British brethren. We have warned them from time to time of attempts by their legislature to extend an unwarrantable jurisdiction over us. We have reminded them of the circumstances of our emigration and settlement here. We have appealed to their native justice and magnanimity, and we have conjured them by the ties of our common kindred to disavow these usurpations, which would inevitably interrupt our connections and correspondence. They too have been deaf to the voice of justice and of consanguinity. We must, therefore, acquiesce in the necessity, which denounces our Separation, and hold them, as we hold the rest of mankind, Enemies in War, in Peace Friends.

We, therefore, the Representatives of the united States of America, in General Congress, Assembled, appealing to the Supreme Judge of the world for the rectitude of our intentions, do, in the Name, and by Authority of the good People of these Colonies, solemnly publish and declare, That these united Colonies are, and of Right ought to be Free and Independent States, that they are Absolved from all Allegiance to the British Crown, and that all political connection between them and the State of Great Britain, is and ought to be totally dissolved; and that as Free and Independent States, they have full Power to levy War, conclude Peace, contract Alliances, establish Commerce, and to do all other Acts and Things which Independent States may of right do. — And for the support of this Declaration, with a firm reliance on the protection of

Divine Providence, we mutually pledge to each other our Lives, our Fortunes, and our sacred Honor.

New Hampshire:

Josiah Bartlett, William Whipple, Matthew Thornton

Massachusetts:

John Hancock, Samuel Adams, John Adams, Robert Treat Paine, Elbridge Gerry

Rhode Island:

Stephen Hopkins, William Ellery

Connecticut:

Roger Sherman, Samuel Huntington, William Williams, Oliver Wolcott

New York:

William Floyd, Philip Livingston, Francis Lewis, Lewis Morris

New Jersey:

Richard Stockton, John Witherspoon, Francis Hopkinson,

John Hart, Abraham Clark

Pennsylvania:

Robert Morris, Benjamin Rush, Benjamin Franklin, John
Morton, George Clymer, James Smith, George Taylor,
James Wilson, George Ross

Delaware:

Caesar Rodney, George Read, Thomas McKean

Maryland:

Samuel Chase, William Paca, Thomas Stone, Charles
Carroll of Carrollton

Virginia:

George Wythe, Richard Henry Lee, Thomas Jefferson,
Benjamin Harrison, Thomas Nelson, Jr., Francis Lightfoot
Lee, Carter Braxton

North Carolina:

William Hooper, Joseph Hewes, John Penn

South Carolina:

Edward Rutledge, Thomas Heyward, Jr., Thomas Lynch, Jr., Arthur Middleton

Georgia:

Button Gwinnett, Lyman Hall, George Walton

http://www.ushistory.org/declaration/document/

The Constitution

We the People of the United States, in Order to form a more perfect Union, establish Justice, insure domestic Tranquility, provide for the common defence, promote the general Welfare, and secure the Blessings of Liberty to ourselves and our Posterity, do ordain and establish this Constitution for the United States of America.

Article 1.

Section 1

All legislative Powers herein granted shall be vested in a

Congress of the United States, which shall consist of a

Senate and House of Representatives.

Section 2

The House of Representatives shall be composed of

Members chosen every second Year by the People of the

several States, and the Electors in each State shall

have the Qualifications requisite for Electors of the most

numerous Branch of the State Legislature.

No Person shall be a Representative who shall not have

attained to the Age of twenty five Years, and been seven

Years a Citizen of the United States, and who shall not,

when elected, be an Inhabitant of that State in which he

shall be chosen.

Representatives and direct Taxes shall be apportioned

among the several States which may be included within this

Union, according to their respective Numbers, which shall

be determined by adding to the whole Number of free

Persons, including those bound to Service for a Term of

Years, and excluding Indians not taxed, three fifths of all

other Persons.

The actual Enumeration shall be made within three Years

after the first Meeting of the Congress of the United States,

and within every subsequent Term of ten Years, in such

Manner as they shall by Law direct. The Number of

Representatives shall not exceed one for every thirty

Thousand, but each State shall have at Least one

Representative; and until such enumeration shall be

made, the State of New Hampshire shall be entitled to

choose three, Massachusetts eight, Rhode Island and

Providence Plantations one, Connecticut five, New York

six, New Jersey four, Pennsylvania eight, Delaware one,

Maryland six, Virginia ten, North Carolina five, South

Carolina five and Georgia three.

When vacancies happen in the Representation from any

State, the Executive Authority thereof shall issue Writs of

Election to fill such Vacancies.

The House of Representatives shall choose their Speaker

and other Officers; and shall have the sole Power of

Impeachment.

Section 3

The Senate of the United States shall be composed of two

Senators from each State, chosen by the Legislature

thereof, for six Years; and each Senator shall

have one Vote.

Immediately after they shall be assembled in Consequence

of the first Election, they shall be divided as equally as may

be into three Classes. The Seats of the Senators of the first

Class shall be vacated at the Expiration of the second

Year, of the second Class at the Expiration of the fourth

Year, and of the third Class at the Expiration of the sixth

Year, so that one third may be chosen every second Year;

and if Vacancies happen by Resignation, or otherwise,

during the Recess of the Legislature of any State, the

Executive thereof may make temporary Appointments until

the next Meeting of the Legislature, which shall then fill

such Vacancies.

No person shall be a Senator who shall not have attained to

the Age of thirty Years, and been nine Years a Citizen of

the United States, and who shall not, when elected, be an

Inhabitant of that State for which he shall be chosen.

The Vice President of the United States shall be President

of the Senate, but shall have no Vote, unless they be equally

divided.

The Senate shall choose their other Officers, and also a

President pro tempore, in the absence of the Vice

President, or when he shall exercise the Office of

President of the United States.

The Senate shall have the sole Power to try all

Impeachments. When sitting for that Purpose, they shall be

on Oath or Affirmation. When the President of the

United States is tried, the Chief Justice shall preside: And no Person shall be convicted without the Concurrence of two thirds of the Members present.

Judgment in Cases of Impeachment shall not extend further than to removal from Office, and disqualification to hold and enjoy any Office of honor, Trust or Profit under the United States: but the Party convicted shall nevertheless be liable and subject to Indictment, Trial, Judgment and Punishment, according to Law.

Section 4

The Times, Places and Manner of holding Elections for Senators and Representatives, shall be prescribed in each State by the Legislature thereof; but the Congress may at any time by Law make or alter such Regulations, except as to the Place of Choosing Senators.

The Congress shall assemble at least once in every Year,
and such Meeting shall be on the first Monday in
December, unless they shall by Law appoint a
different Day.

Section 5

Each House shall be the Judge of the Elections, Returns
and Qualifications of its own Members, and a Majority of
each shall constitute a Quorum to do Business; but a
smaller number may adjourn from day to day, and may be
authorized to compel the Attendance of absent Members,
in such Manner, and under such Penalties as each House
may provide.

Each House may determine the Rules of its Proceedings,
punish its Members for disorderly Behavior, and, with the
Concurrence of two-thirds, expel a Member.

Each House shall keep a Journal of its Proceedings, and from time to time publish the same, excepting such Parts as may in their Judgment require Secrecy; and the Yeas and Nays of the Members of either House on any question shall, at the Desire of one fifth of those Present, be entered on the Journal.

Neither House, during the Session of Congress, shall, without the Consent of the other, adjourn for more than three days, nor to any other Place than that in which the two Houses shall be sitting.

Section 6

The Senators and Representatives shall receive a Compensation for their Services, to be ascertained by Law, and paid out of the Treasury of the United States. They shall in all Cases, except Treason, Felony and Breach of the

Peace, be privileged from Arrest during their Attendance at

the Session of their respective Houses, and in going to and

returning from the same; and for any Speech or Debate in

either House, they shall not be questioned in any other

Place.

No Senator or Representative shall, during the Time for

which he was elected, be appointed to any civil Office

under the Authority of the United States which shall have

been created, or the Emoluments whereof shall have been

increased during such time; and no Person holding any

Office under the United States, shall be a Member of either

House during his Continuance in Office.

Section 7

All bills for raising Revenue shall originate in the House of

Representatives; but the Senate may propose or concur with Amendments as on other Bills.

Every Bill which shall have passed the House of Representatives and the Senate, shall, before it become a Law, be presented to the President of the United States; If he approve he shall sign it, but if not he shall return it, with his Objections to that House in which it shall have originated, who shall enter the Objections at large on their Journal, and proceed to reconsider it. If after such Reconsideration two thirds of that House shall agree to pass the Bill, it shall be sent, together with the Objections, to the other House, by which it shall likewise be reconsidered, and if approved by two thirds of that House, it shall become a Law. But in all such Cases the Votes of both Houses shall be determined by Yeas and Nays, and the Names of the Persons voting for and against the Bill shall be entered on the Journal of each House respectively.

If any Bill shall not be returned by the President within ten

Days (Sundays excepted) after it shall have been presented

to him, the Same shall be a Law, in like Manner as if he had

signed it, unless the Congress by their Adjournment

prevent its Return, in which Case it shall not be a Law.

Every Order, Resolution, or Vote to which the

Concurrence of the Senate and House of Representatives

may be necessary (except on a question of Adjournment)

shall be presented to the President of the United States;

and before the Same shall take Effect, shall be approved by

him, or being disapproved by him, shall be repassed by two

thirds of the Senate and House of Representatives,

according to the Rules and Limitations prescribed in the

Case of a Bill.

Section 8

The Congress shall have Power To lay and collect Taxes, Duties, Imposts and Excises, to pay the Debts and provide for the common Defence and general Welfare of the United States; but all Duties, Imposts and Excises shall be uniform throughout the United States;

To borrow money on the credit of the United States;

To regulate Commerce with foreign Nations, and among the several States, and with the Indian Tribes;

To establish an uniform Rule of Naturalization, and uniform Laws on the subject of Bankruptcies throughout the United States;

To coin Money, regulate the Value thereof, and of foreign Coin, and fix the Standard of Weights and Measures;

To provide for the Punishment of counterfeiting the Securities and current Coin of the United States;

To establish Post Offices and Post Roads;

To promote the Progress of Science and useful Arts, by securing for limited Times to Authors and Inventors the exclusive Right to their respective Writings and Discoveries;

To constitute Tribunals inferior to the supreme Court;

To define and punish Piracies and Felonies committed on the high Seas, and Offenses against the Law of Nations;

To declare War, grant Letters of Marque and Reprisal, and make Rules concerning Captures on Land and Water;

To raise and support Armies, but no Appropriation of Money to that Use shall be for a longer Term than two Years;

To provide and maintain a Navy;

To make Rules for the Government and Regulation of the land and naval Forces;

To provide for calling forth the Militia to execute the Laws of the Union, suppress Insurrections and repel Invasions;

To provide for organizing, arming, and disciplining, the Militia, and for governing such Part of them as may be employed in the Service of the United States, reserving to the States respectively, the Appointment of the Officers, and the Authority of training the Militia according to the discipline prescribed by Congress;

To exercise exclusive Legislation in all Cases whatsoever, over such District (not exceeding ten Miles square) as may, by Cession of particular States, and the acceptance of Congress, become the Seat of the Government of the United States, and to exercise like Authority over all Places purchased by the Consent of the Legislature of the State in which the Same shall be, for the Erection of Forts, Magazines, Arsenals, dock-Yards, and other needful Buildings; And make all Laws which shall be necessary and proper for carrying into Execution the foregoing Powers, and all other Powers vested by this Constitution in the

Government of the United States, or in any Department or

Officer thereof.

Section 9

The Migration or Importation of such Persons as any of

the States now existing shall think proper to admit, shall

not be prohibited by the Congress prior to the Year one

thousand eight hundred and eight, but a tax or duty may be

imposed on such Importation, not exceeding ten dollars for

each Person.

The privilege of the Writ of Habeas Corpus shall not be

suspended, unless when in Cases of Rebellion or Invasion

the public Safety may require it.

No Bill of Attainder or ex post facto Law shall be passed.

No capitation, or other direct, Tax shall be laid, unless in

Proportion to the Census or Enumeration herein before

directed to be taken.

No Tax or Duty shall be laid on Articles exported from any State.

No Preference shall be given by any Regulation of Commerce or Revenue to the Ports of one State over those of another: nor shall Vessels bound to, or from, one State, be obliged to enter, clear, or pay Duties in another.

No Money shall be drawn from the Treasury, but in Consequence of Appropriations made by Law; and a regular Statement and Account of the Receipts and Expenditures of all public Money shall be published from time to time.

No Title of Nobility shall be granted by the United States: And no Person holding any Office of Profit or Trust under them, shall, without the Consent of the Congress, accept of any present, Emolument, Office, or Title, of any kind whatever, from any King, Prince or foreign State.

Section 10

No State shall enter into any Treaty, Alliance, or Confederation; grant Letters of Marque and Reprisal; coin Money; emit Bills of Credit; make any Thing but gold and silver Coin a Tender in Payment of Debts; pass any Bill of Attainder, ex post facto Law, or Law impairing the Obligation of Contracts, or grant any Title of Nobility.

No State shall, without the Consent of the Congress, lay any Imposts or Duties on Imports or Exports, except what may be absolutely necessary for executing its inspection Laws: and the net Produce of all Duties and Imposts, laid by any State on Imports or Exports, shall be for the Use of the Treasury of the United States; and all such Laws shall be subject to the Revision and Control of the Congress.

No State shall, without the Consent of Congress, lay any duty of Tonnage, keep Troops, or Ships of War in time of Peace, enter into any Agreement or Compact with another State, or with a foreign Power, or engage in War, unless actually invaded, or in such imminent Danger as will not admit of delay.

Article 2.

Section 1

The executive Power shall be vested in a President of the United States of America. He shall hold his Office during the Term of four Years, and, together with the Vice-President chosen for the same Term, be elected, as follows:

Each State shall appoint, in such Manner as the Legislature

thcrcof may direct, a Number of Electors, equal to the

whole Number of Senators and Representatives to which

the State may be entitled in the Congress: but no Senator or

Representative, or Person holding an Office of Trust or

Profit under the United States, shall be appointed an

Elector.

The Electors shall meet in their respective States, and vote

by Ballot for two persons, of whom one at least shall not lie

an Inhabitant of the same State with themselves. And they

shall make a List of all the Persons voted for, and of the

Number of Votes for each; which List they shall sign and

certify, and transmit sealed to the Seat of the Government

of the United States, directed to the President of the

Senate. The President of the Senate shall, in the Presence

of the Senate and House of Representatives, open all the

Certificates, and the Votes shall then be counted. The

Person having the greatest Number of Votes shall be the

President, if such Number be a Majority of the whole

Number of Electors appointed; and if there be more than

one who have such Majority, and have an equal Number of

Votes, then the House of Representatives shall immediately

choose by Ballot one of them for President; and if no

Person have a Majority, then from the five highest on the

List the said House shall in like Manner choose the

President. But in choosing the President, the Votes shall be

taken by States, the Representation from each State having

one Vote; a quorum for this Purpose shall consist of a

Member or Members from two-thirds of the States, and a

Majority of all the States shall be necessary to a Choice. In

every Case, after the Choice of the President, the Person

having the greatest Number of Votes of the Electors shall

be the Vice President. But if there should remain two or

more who have equal Votes, the Senate shall choose from

them by Ballot the Vice-President.

The Congress may determine the Time of choosing the

Electors, and the Day on which they shall give their Votes;

which Day shall be the same throughout the United States.

No person except a natural born Citizen, or a Citizen of the

United States, at the time of the Adoption of this

Constitution, shall be eligible to the Office of President;

neither shall any Person be eligible to that Office who shall

not have attained to the Age of thirty-five Years, and been

fourteen Years a Resident within the United States.

In Case of the Removal of the President from Office, or of

his Death, Resignation, or Inability to discharge the Powers

and Duties of the said Office, the same shall devolve on

the Vice President, and the Congress may by Law provide

for the Case of Removal, Death, Resignation or Inability, both of the President and Vice President, declaring what Officer shall then act as President, and such Officer shall act accordingly, until the Disability be removed, or a President shall be elected.

The President shall, at stated Times, receive for his Services, a Compensation, which shall neither be increased nor diminished during the Period for which he shall have been elected, and he shall not receive within that Period any other Emolument from the United States, or any of them.

Before he enter on the Execution of his Office, he shall take the following Oath or Affirmation:

"I do solemnly swear (or affirm) that I will faithfully

execute the Office of President of the United States, and

will to the best of my Ability, preserve, protect and defend

the Constitution of the United States."

Section 2

The President shall be Commander in Chief of the Army

and Navy of the United States, and of the Militia of the

several States, when called into the actual Service of the

United States; he may require the Opinion, in writing, of

the principal Officer in each of the executive Departments,

upon any subject relating to the Duties of their respective

Offices, and he shall have Power to Grant Reprieves and

Pardons for Offenses against the United States, except in

Cases of Impeachment.

He shall have Power, by and with the Advice and Consent

of the Senate, to make Treaties, provided two thirds of the

Senators present concur; and he shall nominate, and by and with the Advice and Consent of the Senate, shall appoint Ambassadors, other public Ministers and Consuls, Judges of the supreme Court, and all other Officers of the United States, whose Appointments are not herein otherwise provided for, and which shall be established by Law: but the Congress may by Law vest the Appointment of such inferior Officers, as they think proper, in the President alone, in the Courts of Law, or in the Heads of Departments.

The President shall have Power to fill up all Vacancies that may happen during the Recess of the Senate, by granting Commissions which shall expire at the End of their next Session.

Section 3

He shall from time to time give to the Congress Information of the State of the Union, and recommend to their Consideration such Measures as he shall judge necessary and expedient; he may, on extraordinary Occasions, convene both Houses, or either of them, and in Case of Disagreement between them, with Respect to the Time of Adjournment, he may adjourn them to such Time as he shall think proper; he shall receive Ambassadors and other public Ministers; he shall take Care that the Laws be faithfully executed, and shall Commission all the Officers of the United States.

Section 4

The President, Vice President and all civil Officers of the United States, shall be removed from Office on Impeachment for, and Conviction of, Treason, Bribery, or other high Crimes and Misdemeanors.

Article 3.

Section 1

The judicial Power of the United States, shall be vested in one supreme Court, and in such inferior Courts as the Congress may from time to time ordain and establish. The Judges, both of the supreme and inferior Courts, shall hold their Offices during good Behavior, and shall, at stated Times, receive for their Services a Compensation which shall not be diminished during their Continuance in Office.

Section 2

The judicial Power shall extend to all Cases, in Law and Equity, arising under this Constitution, the Laws of the United States, and Treaties made, or which shall be made, under their Authority; to all Cases affecting Ambassadors, other public Ministers and Consuls; to all Cases of

admiralty and maritime Jurisdiction; to Controversies to

which the United States shall be a Party; to Controversies

between two or more States; between a State and Citizens

of another State; between Citizens of different States;

between Citizens of the same State claiming Lands under

Grants of different States, and between a State, or the

Citizens thereof, and foreign States, Citizens or Subjects.

In all Cases affecting Ambassadors, other public Ministers

and Consuls, and those in which a State shall be Party, the

supreme Court shall have original Jurisdiction. In all the

other Cases before mentioned, the supreme Court shall

have appellate Jurisdiction, both as to Law and Fact, with

such Exceptions, and under such Regulations as the

Congress shall make.

The Trial of all Crimes, except in Cases of Impeachment, shall be by Jury; and such Trial shall be held in the State where the said Crimes shall have been committed; but when not committed within any State, the Trial shall be at such Place or Places as the Congress may by Law have directed.

Section 3

Treason against the United States, shall consist only in levying War against them, or in adhering to their Enemies, giving them Aid and Comfort. No Person shall be convicted of Treason unless on the Testimony of two Witnesses to the same overt Act, or on Confession in open Court.

The Congress shall have power to declare the Punishment of Treason, but no Attainder of Treason shall work

Corruption of Blood, or Forfeiture except during the Life of the Person attainted.

Article 4.

Section 1

Full Faith and Credit shall be given in each State to the public Acts, Records, and judicial Proceedings of every other State. And the Congress may by general Laws prescribe the Manner in which such Acts, Records and Proceedings shall be proved, and the Effect thereof.

Section 2

The Citizens of each State shall be entitled to all Privileges and Immunities of Citizens in the several States.

A Person charged in any State with Treason, Felony, or

other Crime, who shall flee from Justice, and be found in another State, shall on demand of the executive Authority of the State from which he fled, be delivered up, to be removed to the State having Jurisdiction of the Crime.

No Person held to Service or Labour in one State, under the Laws thereof, escaping into another, shall, in Consequence of any Law or Regulation therein, be discharged from such Service or Labour, But shall be delivered up on Claim of the Party to whom such Service or Labour may be due.

Section 3

New States may be admitted by the Congress into this Union; but no new States shall be formed or erected within the Jurisdiction of any other State; nor any State be formed by the Junction of two or more States, or parts of States, without the Consent of the Legislatures of the States

concerned as well as of the Congress.

The Congress shall have Power to dispose of and make all

needful Rules and Regulations respecting the Territory or

other Property belonging to the United States; and nothing

in this Constitution shall be so construed as to Prejudice

any Claims of the United States, or of any particular State.

Section 4

The United States shall guarantee to every State in this

Union a Republican Form of Government, and shall

protect each of them against Invasion; and on Application

of the Legislature, or of the Executive (when the

Legislature cannot be convened) against domestic Violence.

Article 5.

The Congress, whenever two thirds of both Houses shall deem it necessary, shall propose Amendments to this Constitution, or, on the Application of the Legislatures of two thirds of the several States, shall call a Convention for proposing Amendments, which, in either Case, shall be valid to all Intents and Purposes, as part of this Constitution, when ratified by the Legislatures of three fourths of the several States, or by Conventions in three fourths thereof, as the one or the other Mode of Ratification may be proposed by the Congress; Provided that no Amendment which may be made prior to the Year One thousand eight hundred and eight shall in any Manner affect the first and fourth Clauses in the Ninth Section of the first Article; and that no State, without its Consent, shall be deprived of its equal Suffrage in the Senate.

Article 6.

All Debts contracted and Engagements entered into, before the Adoption of this Constitution, shall be as valid against the United States under this Constitution, as under the Confederation.

This Constitution, and the Laws of the United States which shall be made in Pursuance thereof; and all Treaties made, or which shall be made, under the Authority of the United States, shall be the supreme Law of the Land; and the Judges in every State shall be bound thereby, any Thing in the Constitution or Laws of any State to the Contrary notwithstanding.

The Senators and Representatives before mentioned, and the Members of the several State Legislatures, and all executive and judicial Officers, both of the United States

and of the several States, shall be bound by Oath or

Affirmation, to support this Constitution; but no religious

Test shall ever be required as a Qualification to any Office

or public Trust under the United

States.

Article 7.

The Ratification of the Conventions of nine States, shall be

sufficient for the Establishment of this Constitution

between the States so ratifying the Same.

Done in Convention by the Unanimous Consent of the

States present the Seventeenth Day of September in the

Year of our Lord one thousand seven hundred

and Eighty seven and of the Independence of the United

States of America the Twelfth. In Witness whereof We

have hereunto subscribed our Names.

George Washington - President and deputy from Virginia

New Hampshire - John Langdon, Nicholas Gilman

Massachusetts - Nathaniel Gorham, Rufus King

Connecticut - William Samuel Johnson, Roger Sherman

New York - Alexander Hamilton

New Jersey - William Livingston, David Brearley, William

Paterson, Jonathan

Dayton

Pennsylvania - Benjamin Franklin, Thomas Mifflin, Robert Morris, George Clymer,

Thomas Fitzsimons, Jared Ingersoll, James Wilson, Gouvernour Morris

Delaware - George Read, Gunning Bedford Jr., John Dickinson, Richard Bassett,

Jacob Broom

Maryland - James McHenry, Daniel of St Thomas Jenifer, Daniel Carroll

Virginia - John Blair, James Madison Jr.

North Carolina - William Blount, Richard Dobbs Spaight, Hugh Williamson

South Carolina - John Rutledge, Charles Cotesworth

Pinckney, Charles Pinckney,

Pierce Butler

Georgia - William Few, Abraham Baldwin

Attest: William Jackson, Secretary

Amendment 1

Congress shall make no law respecting an establishment of

religion, or prohibiting the free exercise thereof; or

abridging the freedom of speech, or of the press; or the

right of the people peaceably to assemble, and to petition

the Government for a redress of grievances.

Amendment 2

A well regulated Militia, being necessary to the security of a free State, the right of the people to keep and bear Arms, shall not be infringed.

Amendment 3

No Soldier shall, in time of peace be quartered in any house, without the consent of the Owner, nor in time of war, but in a manner to be prescribed by law.

Amendment 4

The right of the people to be secure in their persons, houses, papers, and effects, against unreasonable searches and seizures, shall not be violated, and no Warrants shall issue, but upon probable cause, supported by Oath or affirmation, and particularly describing the place to be searched, and the persons or things to be seized.

Amendment 5

No person shall be held to answer for a capital, or

otherwise infamous crime, unless on a presentment or

indictment of a Grand Jury, except in cases arising

in the land or naval forces, or in the Militia, when in actual

service in time of War or public danger; nor shall any

person be subject for the same offense

to be twice put in jeopardy of life or limb; nor shall be

compelled in any criminal case to be a witness against

himself, nor be deprived of life, liberty, or property,

without due process of law; nor shall private property be

taken for public use, without just compensation.

Amendment 6

In all criminal prosecutions, the accused shall enjoy the

right to a speedy and public trial, by an impartial jury of the

State and district wherein the crime shall have been

committed, which district shall have been previously ascertained by law, and to be informed of the nature and cause of the accusation; to be confronted with the witnesses against him; to have compulsory process for obtaining witnesses in his favor, and to have the Assistance of Counsel for his defence.

Amendment 7

In Suits at common law, where the value in controversy shall exceed twenty dollars, the right of trial by jury shall be preserved, and no fact tried by a jury, shall be otherwise re-examined in any Court of the United States, than according to the rules of the common law.

Amendment 8

Excessive bail shall not be required, nor excessive fines imposed, nor cruel and unusual punishments inflicted.

Amendment 9

The enumeration in the Constitution, of certain rights, shall

not be construed to deny or disparage others retained by

the people.

Amendment 10

The powers not delegated to the United States by the

Constitution, nor prohibited by it to the States, are reserved

to the States respectively, or to the people.

Amendment 11

The Judicial power of the United States shall not be

construed to extend to any suit in law or equity,

commenced or prosecuted against one of the United States

by Citizens of another State, or by Citizens or Subjects of

any Foreign State.

Amendment 12

The Electors shall meet in their respective states, and vote by ballot for President and Vice-President, one of whom, at least, shall not be an inhabitant of the same state with themselves; they shall name in their ballots the person voted for as President, and in distinct ballots the person voted for as Vice-President, and they shall make distinct lists of all persons voted for as President, and of all persons voted for as Vice-President and of the number of votes for each, which lists they shall sign and certify, and transmit sealed to the seat of the government of the United States, directed to the President of the Senate;

The President of the Senate shall, in the presence of the Senate and House of Representatives, open all the certificates and the votes shall then be counted;

The person having the greatest Number of votes for

President, shall be the President, if such number be a

majority of the whole number of Electors appointed; and if

no person have such majority, then from the persons

having the highest numbers not exceeding three on the list

of those voted for as President, the House of

Representatives shall choose immediately, by ballot,

the President. But in choosing the President, the votes shall

be taken by states, the representation from each state

having one vote; a quorum for this purpose shall consist of

a member or members from two-thirds of the states, and

a majority of all the states shall be necessary to a choice.

And if the House of Representatives shall not choose a

President whenever the right of choice shall devolve upon

them, before the fourth day of March next following, then

the Vice-President shall act as President, as in the case of the death or other constitutional disability of the President.

The person having the greatest number of votes as Vice-President, shall be the Vice-President, if such number be a majority of the whole number of Electors appointed, and if no person have a majority, then from the two highest numbers on the list, the Senate shall choose the Vice-President; a quorum for the purpose shall consist of two-thirds of the whole number of Senators, and a majority of the whole number shall be necessary to a choice. But no person constitutionally ineligible to the office of President shall be eligible to that of Vice-President of the United States.

Amendment 13

1. Neither slavery nor involuntary servitude, except as a punishment for crime whereof the party shall have been

duly convicted, shall exist within the United

States, or any place subject to their jurisdiction.

2. Congress shall have power to enforce this article by

appropriate legislation.

Amendment 14

1. All persons born or naturalized in the United States, and

subject to the jurisdiction thereof, are citizens of the United

States and of the State wherein they reside. No State shall

make or enforce any law which shall abridge the privileges

or immunities of citizens of the United States; nor shall any

State deprive any person of life, liberty, or property,

without due process of law; nor deny to any person within

its jurisdiction the equal protection of the laws.

2. Representatives shall be apportioned among the several

States according to their respective numbers, counting the whole number of persons in each State, excluding Indians not taxed. But when the right to vote at any election for the choice of electors for President and Vice-President of the United States, Representatives in Congress, the Executive and Judicial officers of a State, or the members of the Legislature thereof, is denied to any of the male inhabitants of such State, being twenty-one years of age, and citizens of the United States, or in any way abridged, except for participation in rebellion, or other crime, the basis of representation therein shall be reduced in the proportion which the number of such male citizens shall bear to the whole number of male citizens twenty-one years of age in such State.

3. No person shall be a Senator or Representative in Congress, or elector of President and Vice-President, or

hold any office, civil or military, under the United States, or

under any State, who, having previously taken an oath, as a

member of Congress, or as an officer of the United States,

or as a member of any State legislature, or as an executive

or judicial officer of any State, to support the Constitution

of the United States, shall have engaged in insurrection or

rebellion against the same, or given aid or comfort to the

enemies thereof. But Congress may by a vote of two-thirds

of each House, remove such disability.

4. The validity of the public debt of the United States,

authorized by law, including debts incurred for payment of

pensions and bounties for services in suppressing

insurrection or rebellion, shall not be questioned. But

neither the United States nor any State shall assume or pay

any debt or obligation incurred in aid of insurrection or

rebellion against the United States, or any claim for

the loss or emancipation of any slave; but all such debts, obligations and claims shall be held illegal and void.

5. The Congress shall have power to enforce, by appropriate legislation, the provisions of this article.

Amendment 15

1. The right of citizens of the United States to vote shall not be denied or abridged by the United States or by any State on account of race, color, or previous condition of servitude.

2. The Congress shall have power to enforce this article by appropriate legislation.

Amendment 16

The Congress shall have power to lay and collect taxes on

incomes, from whatever source derived, without

apportionment among the several States, and without

regard to any census or enumeration.

Amendment 17

The Senate of the United States shall be composed of two

Senators from each State, elected by the people thereof, for

six years; and each Senator shall have one vote. The

electors in each State shall have the qualifications requisite

for electors of the most numerous branch of the State

legislatures.

When vacancies happen in the representation of any State

in the Senate, the executive authority of such State shall

issue writs of election to fill such vacancies: Provided, That

the legislature of any State may empower the executive

thereof to make temporary appointments until the people

fill the vacancies by election as the legislature may direct.

This amendment shall not be so construed as to affect the election or term of any Senator chosen before it becomes valid as part of the Constitution.

Amendment 18

1. After one year from the ratification of this article the manufacture, sale, or transportation of intoxicating liquors within, the importation thereof into, or the exportation thereof from the United States and all territory subject to the jurisdiction thereof for beverage purposes is hereby prohibited.

2. The Congress and the several States shall have concurrent power to enforce this article by appropriate legislation.

3. This article shall be inoperative unless it shall have been ratified as an amendment to the Constitution by the legislatures of the several States, as provided in the Constitution, within seven years from the date of the submission hereof to the States by the Congress.

Amendment 19

The right of citizens of the United States to vote shall not be denied or abridged by the United States or by any State on account of sex.

Congress shall have power to enforce this article by appropriate legislation.

Amendment 20

1. The terms of the President and Vice President shall end

at noon on the 20th day of January, and the terms of Senators and Representatives at noon on the 3d day of January, of the years in which such terms would have ended if this article had not been ratified; and the terms of their successors shall then begin.

2. The Congress shall assemble at least once in every year, and such meeting shall begin at noon on the 3d day of January, unless they shall by law appoint a different day.

3. If, at the time fixed for the beginning of the term of the President, the President elect shall have died, the Vice President elect shall become President. If a President shall not have been chosen before the time fixed for the beginning of his term, or if the President elect shall have failed to qualify, then the Vice President elect shall act as President until a President shall have qualified; and the

Congress may by law provide for the case wherein

neither a President elect nor a Vice President elect shall

have qualified, declaring who shall then act as President, or

the manner in which one who is to act shall be selected,

and such person shall act accordingly until a President or

Vice President shall have qualified.

4. The Congress may by law provide for the case of the

death of any of the persons from whom the House of

Representatives may choose a President whenever the right

of choice shall have devolved upon them, and for the case

of the death of any of the persons from whom the Senate

may choose a Vice President whenever the right of choice

shall have devolved upon them.

5. Sections 1 and 2 shall take effect on the 15th day of

October following the ratification of this article.

6. This article shall be inoperative unless it shall have been ratified as an amendment to the Constitution by the legislatures of three-fourths of the several States within seven years from the date of its submission.

Amendment 21

1. The eighteenth article of amendment to the Constitution of the United States is hereby repealed.

2. The transportation or importation into any State, Territory, or possession of the United States for delivery or use therein of intoxicating liquors, in violation of the laws thereof, is hereby prohibited.

3. The article shall be inoperative unless it shall have been ratified as an amendment to the Constitution by

conventions in the several States, as provided in the

Constitution, within seven years from the date of the

submission hereof to the States by the Congress.

Amendment 22

1. No person shall be elected to the office of the President

more than twice, and no person who has held the office of

President, or acted as President, for more than two years of

a term to which some other person was elected President

shall be elected to the office of the President more than

once. But this Article shall not apply to any person holding

the office of President, when this Article was proposed by

the Congress, and shall not prevent any person who may

be holding the office of President, or acting as President,

during the term within which this Article becomes

operative from holding the office of President or acting as

President during the remainder of such term.

2. This article shall be inoperative unless it shall have been ratified as an amendment to the Constitution by the legislatures of three-fourths of the several States within seven years from the date of its submission to the States by the Congress.

Amendment 23

1. The District constituting the seat of Government of the United States shall appoint in such manner as the Congress may direct: A number of electors of President and Vice President equal to the whole number of Senators and Representatives in Congress to which the District would be entitled if it were a State, but in no event more than the least populous State; they shall be in addition to those appointed by the States, but they shall be considered, for the purposes of the election of President and Vice

President, to be electors appointed by a State; and they

shall meet in the District and perform such duties as

provided by the twelfth article of amendment.

2. The Congress shall have power to enforce this article by

appropriate legislation.

Amendment 24

1. The right of citizens of the United States to vote in any

primary or other election for President or Vice President,

for electors for President or Vice President, or for Senator

or Representative in Congress, shall not be denied or

abridged by the United States or any State by reason of

failure to pay any poll tax or other tax.

2. The Congress shall have power to enforce this article by

appropriate legislation.

Amendment 25

1. In case of the removal of the President from office or of his death or resignation, the Vice President shall become President.

2. Whenever there is a vacancy in the office of the Vice President, the President shall nominate a Vice President who shall take office upon confirmation by a majority vote of both Houses of Congress.

3. Whenever the President transmits to the President pro tempore of the Senate and the Speaker of the House of Representatives his written declaration that he is unable to discharge the powers and duties of his office, and until he transmits to them a written declaration to the contrary, such powers and duties shall be discharged by the Vice

President as Acting President.

4. Whenever the Vice President and a majority of either the
principal officers of the executive departments or of such
other body as Congress may by law provide, transmit to the
President pro tempore of the Senate and the Speaker of
the House of Representatives their written declaration that
the President is unable to discharge the powers and duties
of his office, the Vice President shall immediately assume
the powers and duties of the office as Acting President.

Thereafter, when the President transmits to the President
pro tempore of the Senate and the Speaker of the House of
Representatives his written declaration that no inability
exists, he shall resume the powers and duties of his office
unless the Vice President and a majority of either the
principal officers of the executive department or of such

other body as Congress may by law provide, transmit

within four days to the President pro tempore of the Senate

and the Speaker of the House of Representatives their

written declaration that the President is unable to discharge

the powers and duties of his office. Thereupon Congress

shall decide the issue, assembling within forty eight hours

for that purpose if not in session. If the Congress, within

twenty one days after receipt of the latter written

declaration, or, if Congress is not in session, within twenty

one days after Congress is required to assemble, determines

by two thirds vote of both Houses that the President is

unable to discharge the powers and duties of his office, the

Vice President shall continue to discharge the same as

Acting President; otherwise, the President shall resume the

powers and duties of his office.

Amendment 26

1. The right of citizens of the United States, who are eighteen years of age or older, to vote shall not be denied or abridged by the United States or by any State on account of age.

2. The Congress shall have power to enforce this article by appropriate legislation.

Amendment 27

No law, varying the compensation for the services of the Senators and Representatives, shall take effect, until an election of Representatives shall have intervened.

https://www.usconstitution.net/const.txt

11 EPILOGUE

Now you will not be able to say to your kids, "I'm sorry, I just did not know what to do," if that time comes, when they look at you and say, "Why didn't you do something, when you had the time and the resources, to stop America's slide into socialism?" I hope you will join me and the other conservative Americans who have been trying to create the conservative takeover of the Republican Party as I have outlined in my earlier eBook and which was further outlined and explained in the last two chapters of Richard Viguerie's book *TAKEOVER: The 100-Year War for the Soul of the GOP and How Conservatives Can Finally Win It.*

On behalf of my family, I thank in advance all of those who purchased this book and have decided to try to become a precinct committeeman where they live and, if for whatever valid reason they cannot become a precinct committeeman, have attempted to recruit others to fill up all the vacant Republican Party precinct committeeman slots across America's voting precincts.

Thank you again.

Daniel J. Schultz

ABOUT THE AUTHOR

Daniel J. Schultz is an elected Arizona Republican Party precinct committeeman and state committeeman, a veteran, an attorney, and an author. He has co-hosted a radio program in the mid-1990s in Los Angeles and was the President of The Lawyer's Second Amendment Society. United States Military Academy graduate. Mr. Schultz served as a U. S. Army Counterintelligence Officer and Human Intelligence Officer, with five years of active duty and eleven years of reserve duty in classified intelligence collection operations. He held a Top Secret security clearance with Special Compartmented Intelligence access.

As a trial attorney, he has both criminal and civil trial experience. He represented insurance policyholders that included Fortune 500 companies and a state government, resulting in making of new, favorable case law for insurance policyholders and recovery of over $175 million for clients. Mr. Schultz has over ten years' of "in the trenches" experience in all aspects of political party governance and campaigns for both political party and public office candidates, including the successful election of a conservative chairman of the Arizona Republican Party and a conservative Republican victory in a primary over an incumbent non-conservative in a state legislature senate race. Mr. Schultz also provided one-on-one campaign advice to a prominent 2012 Republican presidential primary candidate. His first book on The Neighborhood Precinct Committeeman Strategy was aptly named "Taking Back Your Government: The Neighborhood Precinct

Committeeman Strategy," published at the lowest price

possible for an ebook on Amazon.com. That ebook lead

to his winning one-half of Conservative HQ's The Liberty

Prize in 2013 and was featured in Richard Viguerie's book

Takeover: The 100-Year War For The Soul Of The GOP And

How Conservatives Can Finally Win It for answering the

question of how do we conservatives change things and

take over the Republican Party to make it the political

home of limited-government constitutional conservatives

and govern America according to conservative principles in

2017.

Made in the USA
Coppell, TX
11 March 2021